ENJOY COLORING!!

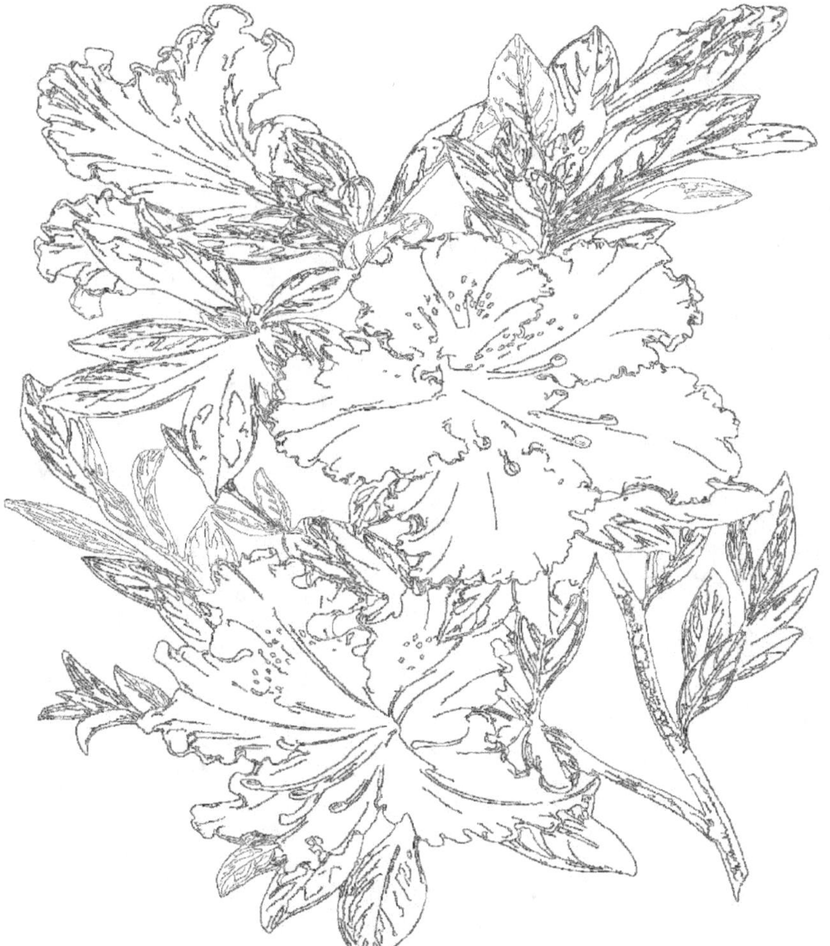

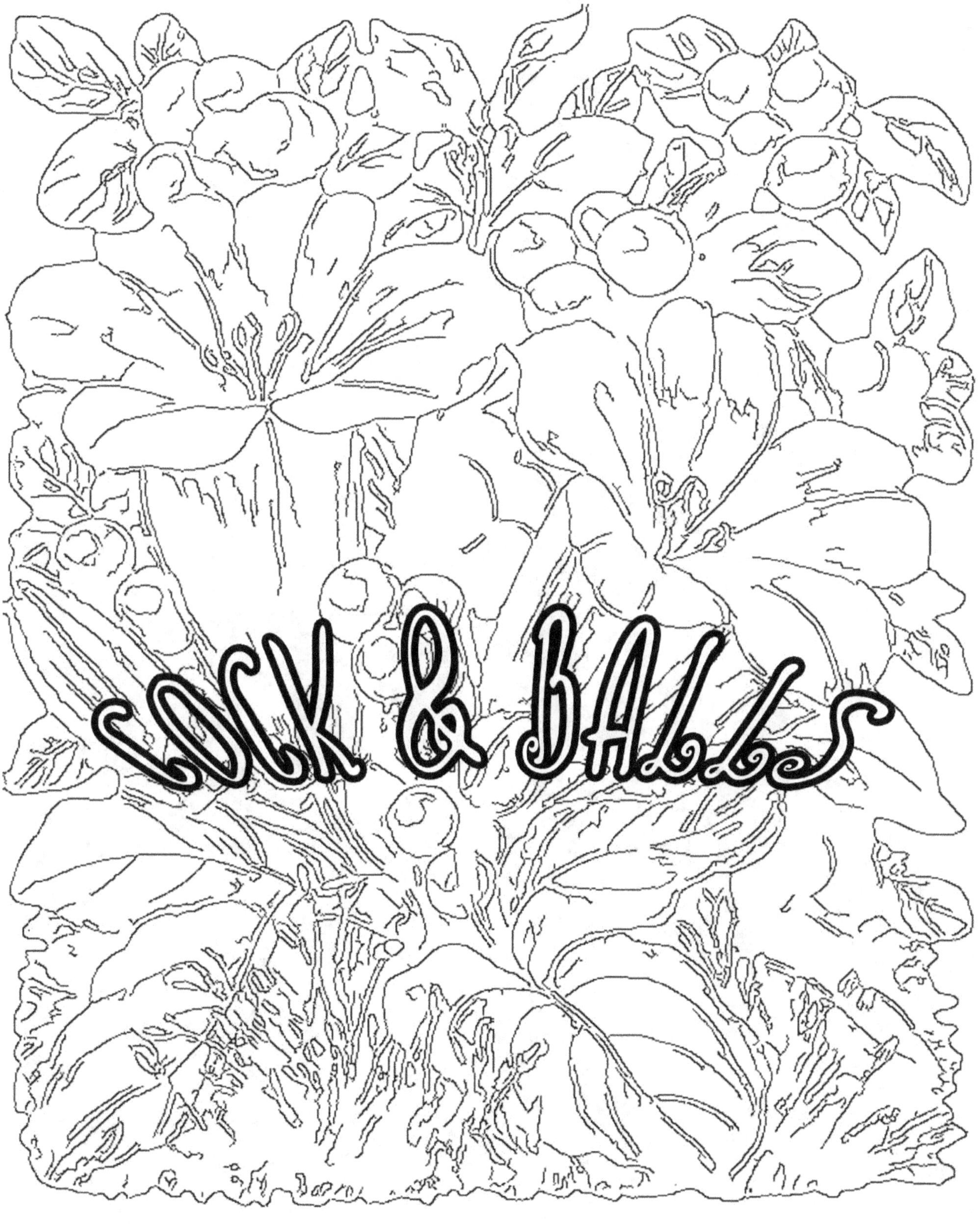
COCK & BALLS

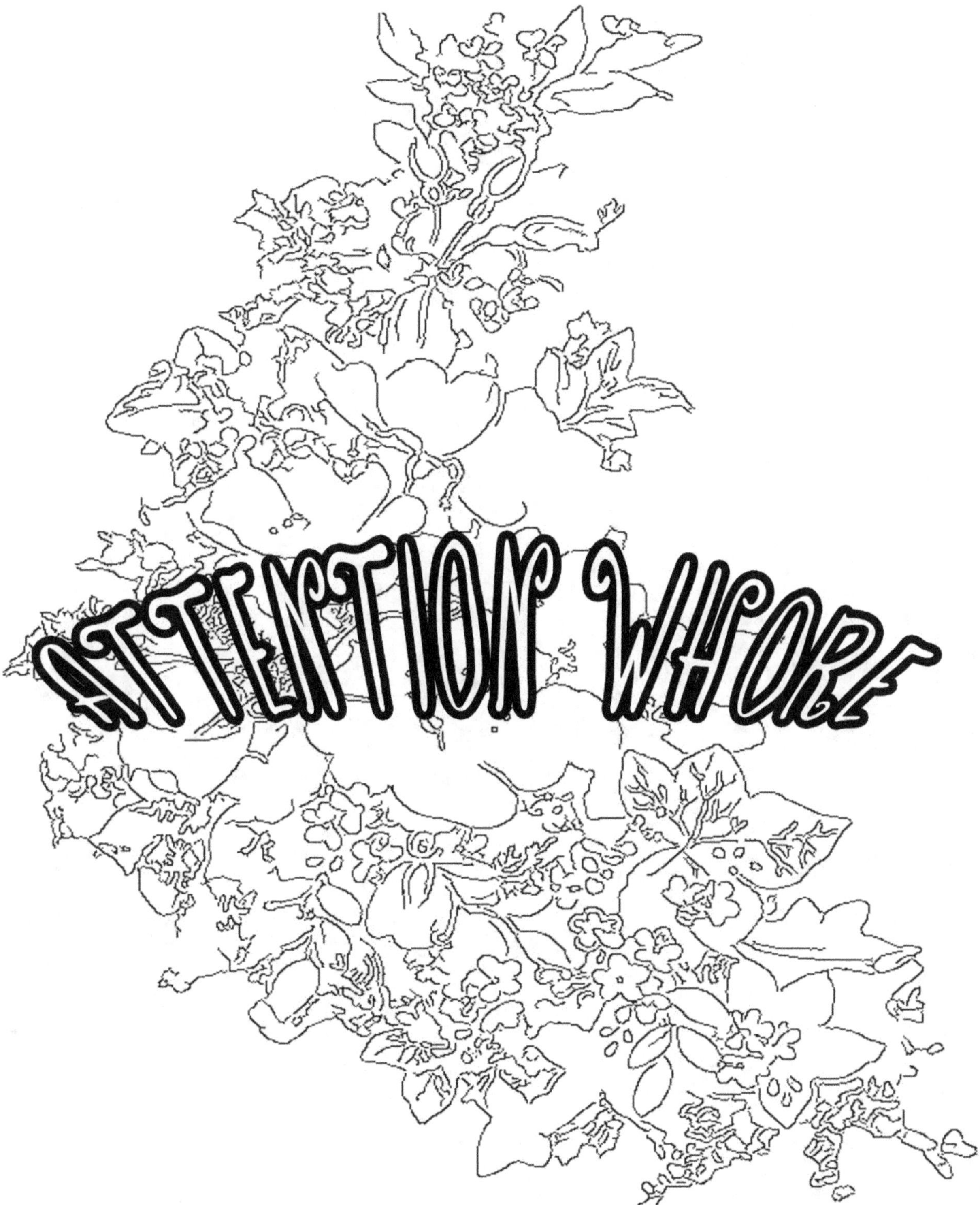
ATTENTION WHORE

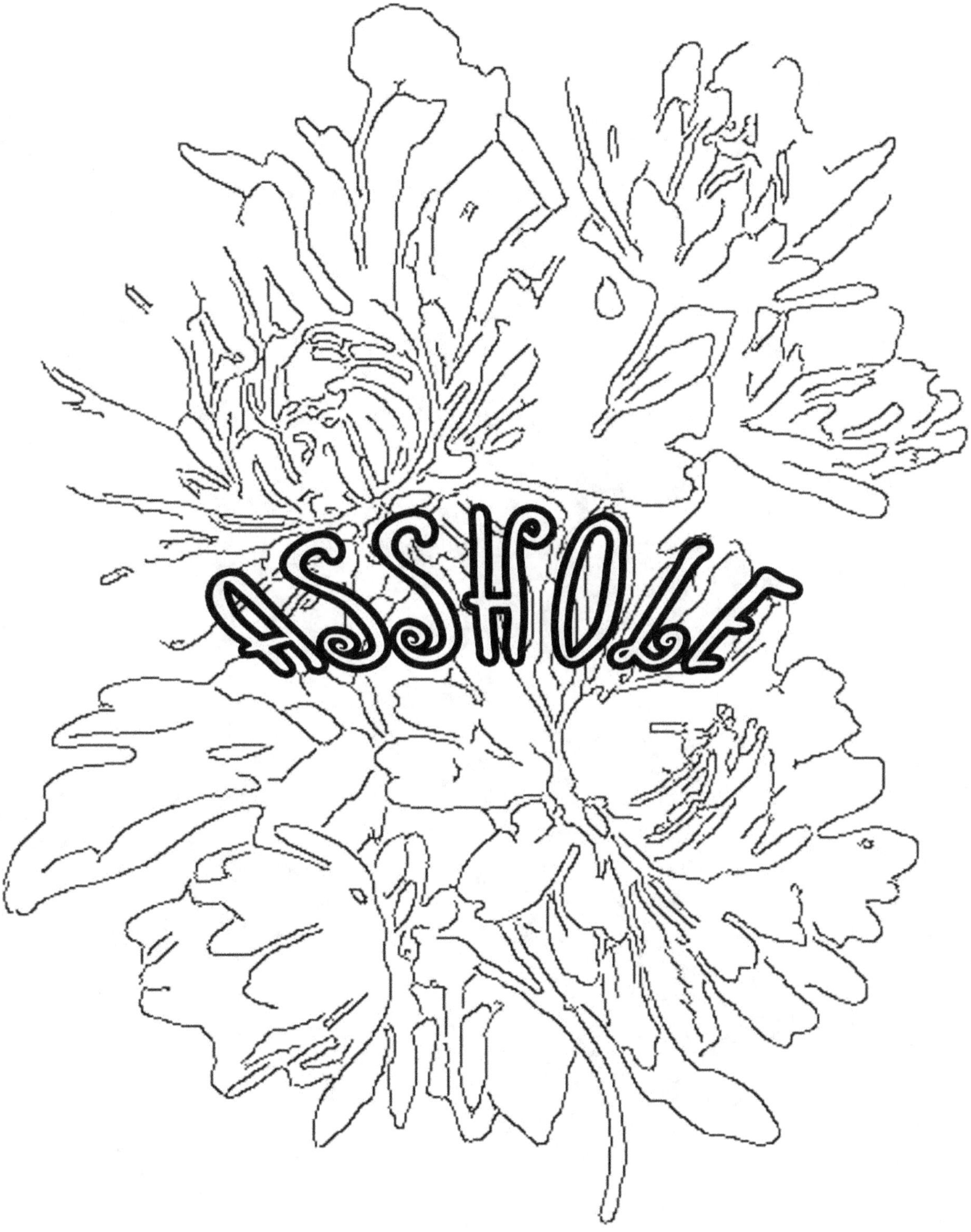
ASSHOLE

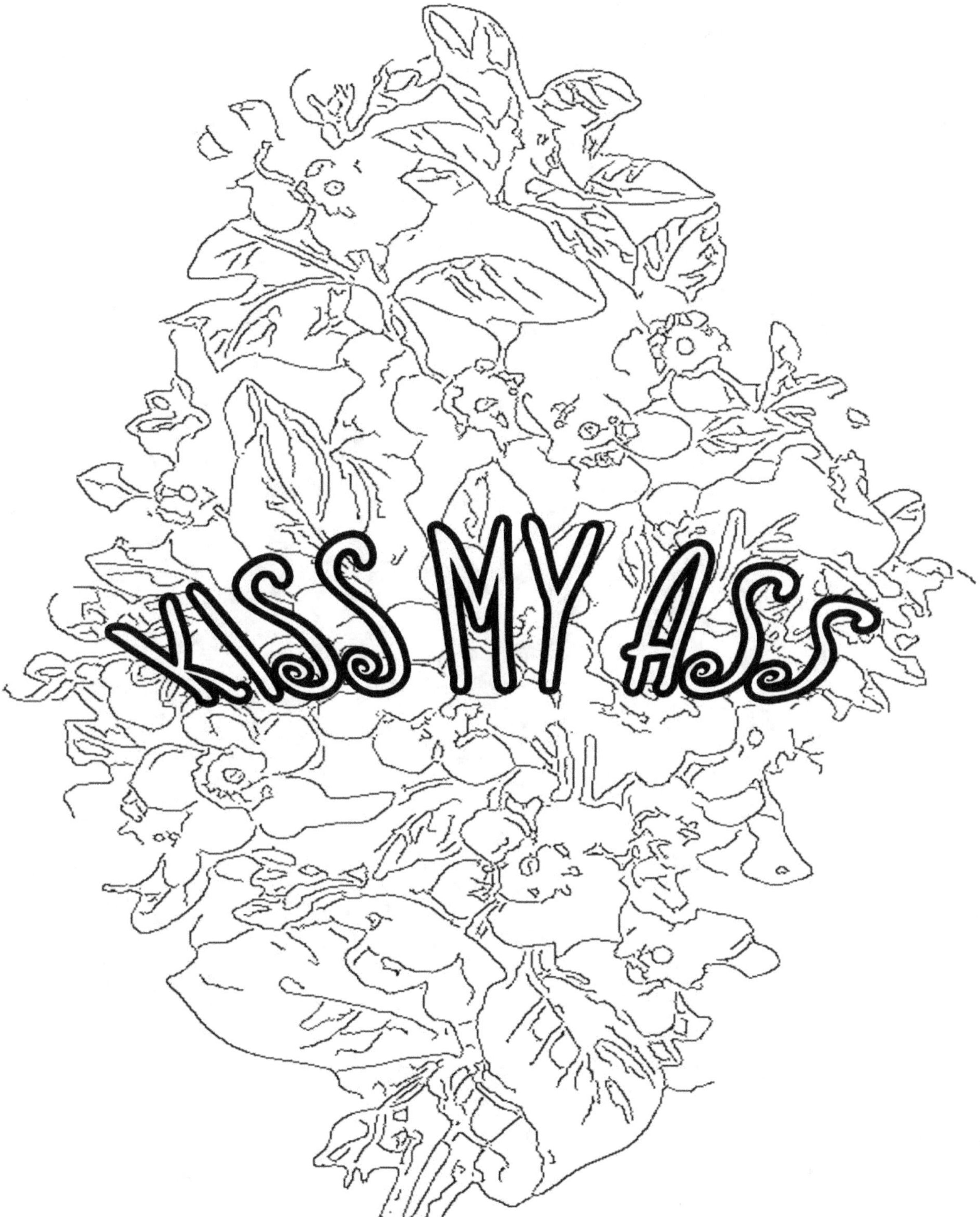
KISS MY ASS

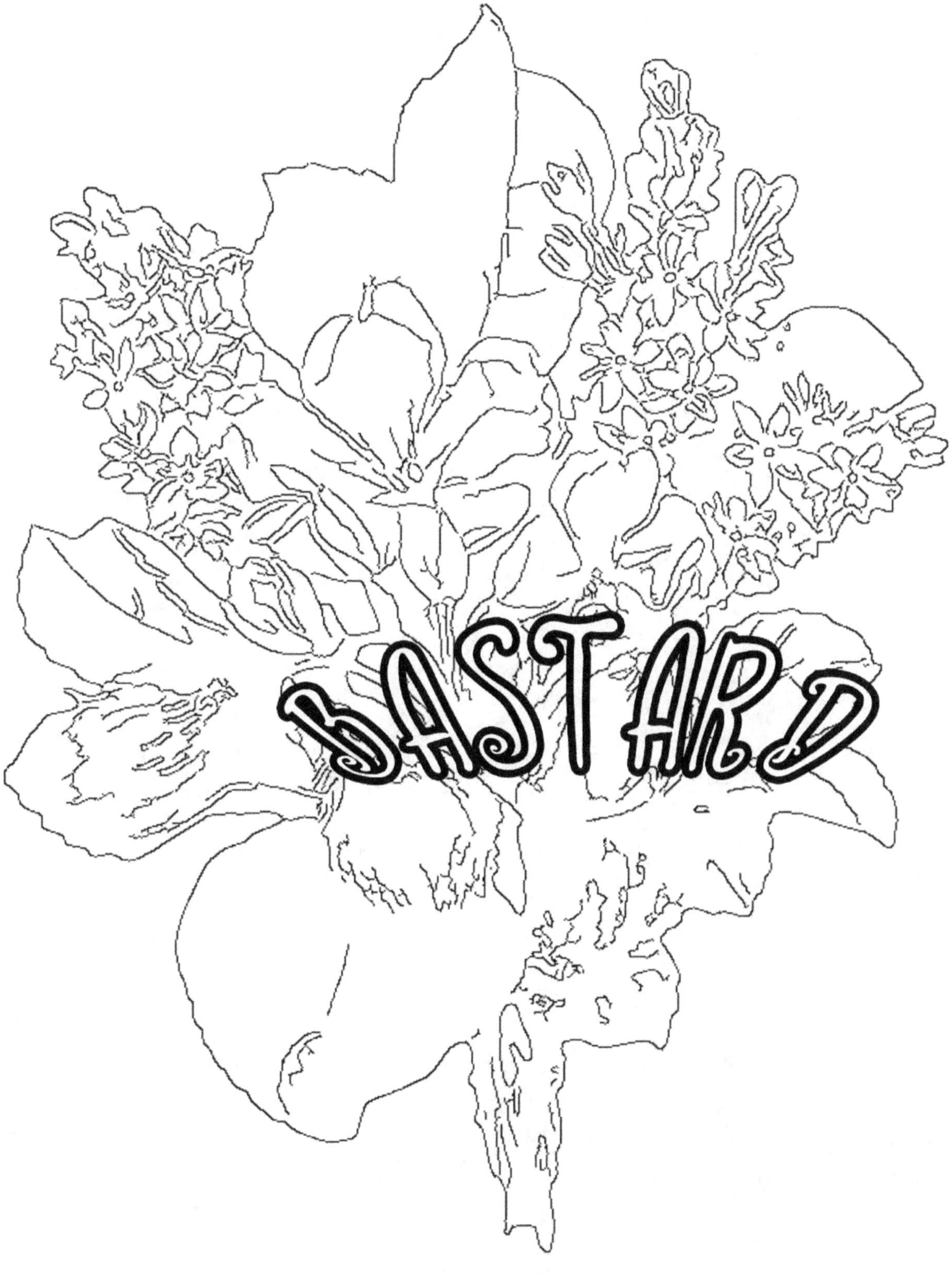
BASTARD

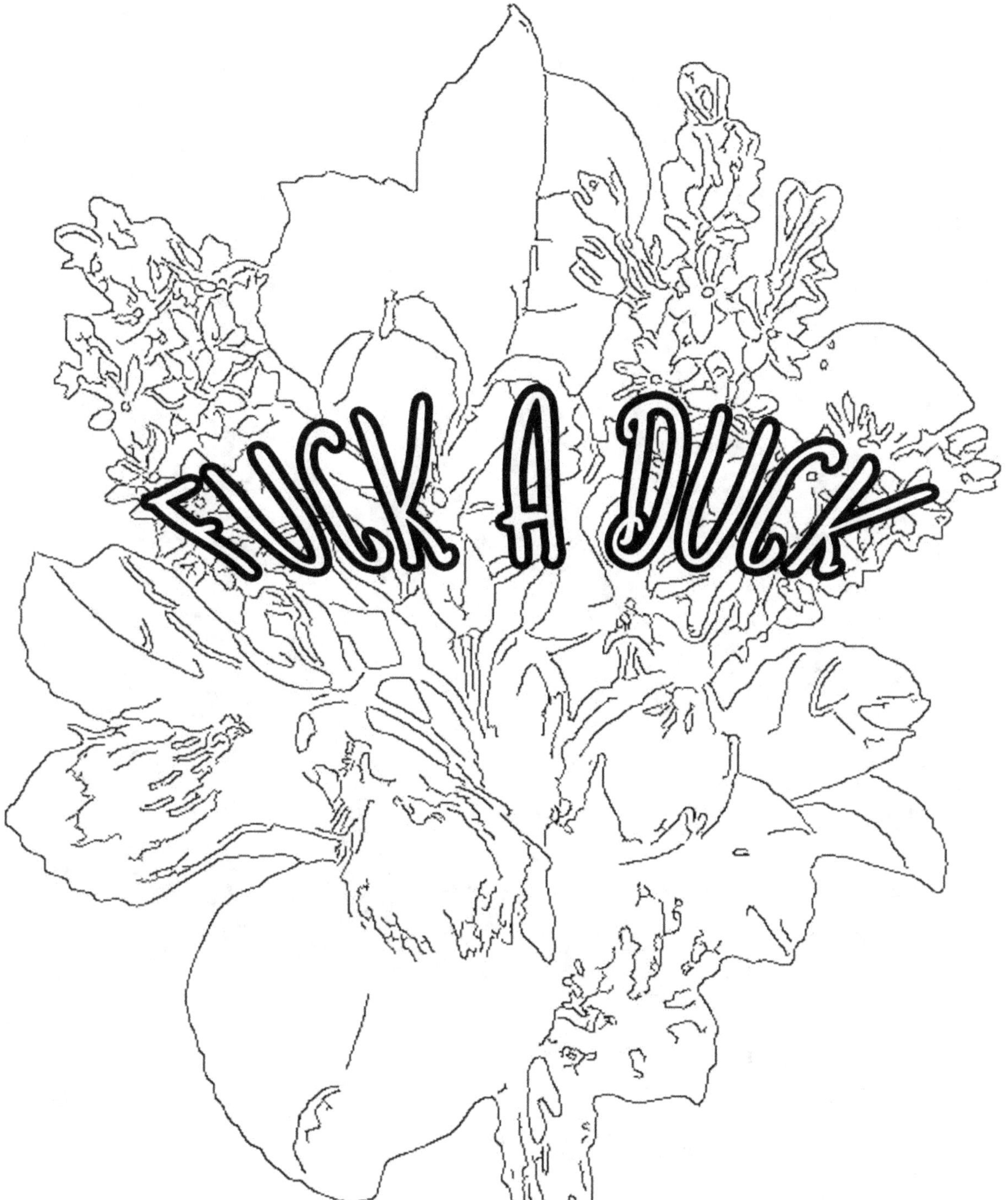
FUCK A DUCK

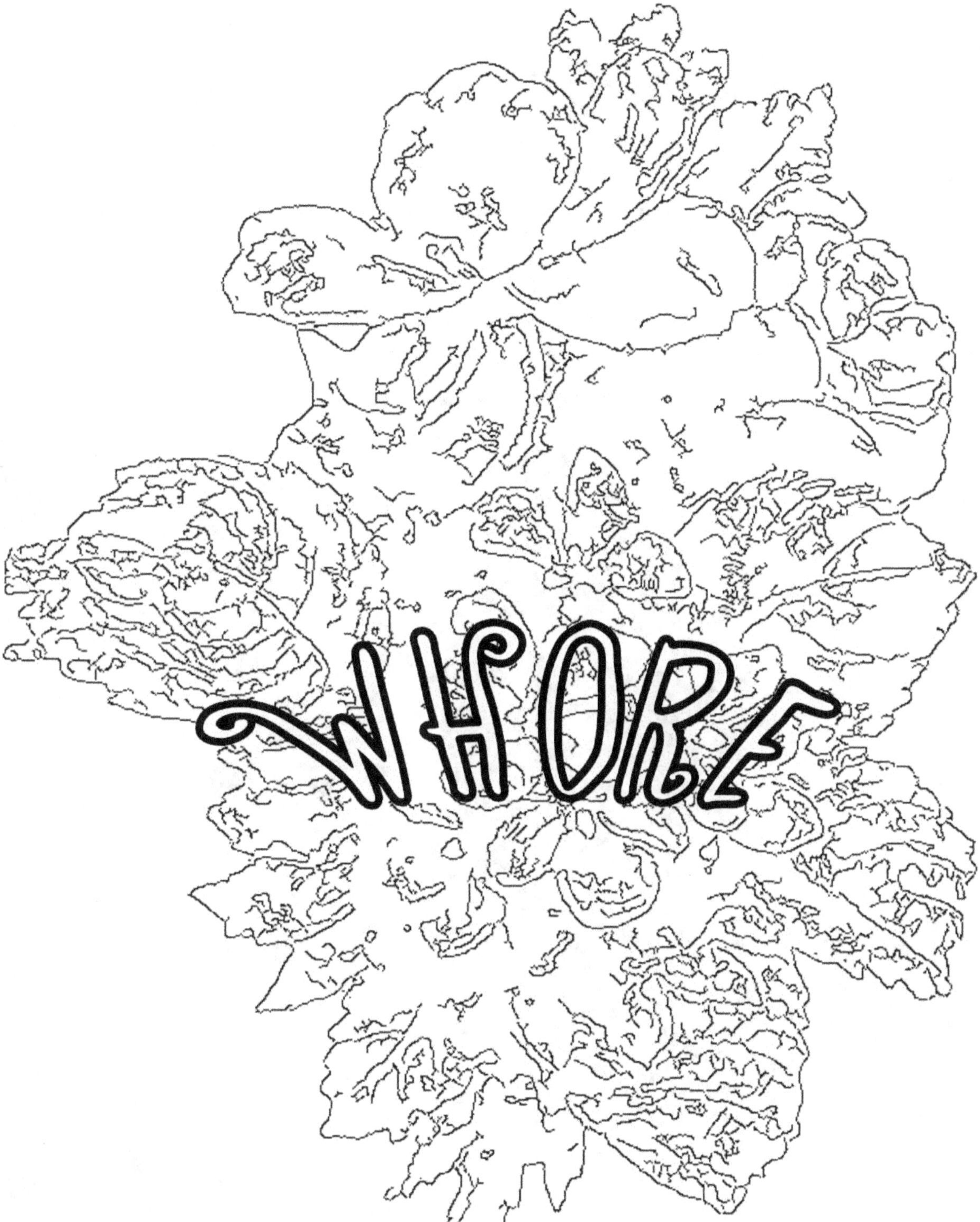
WHORE

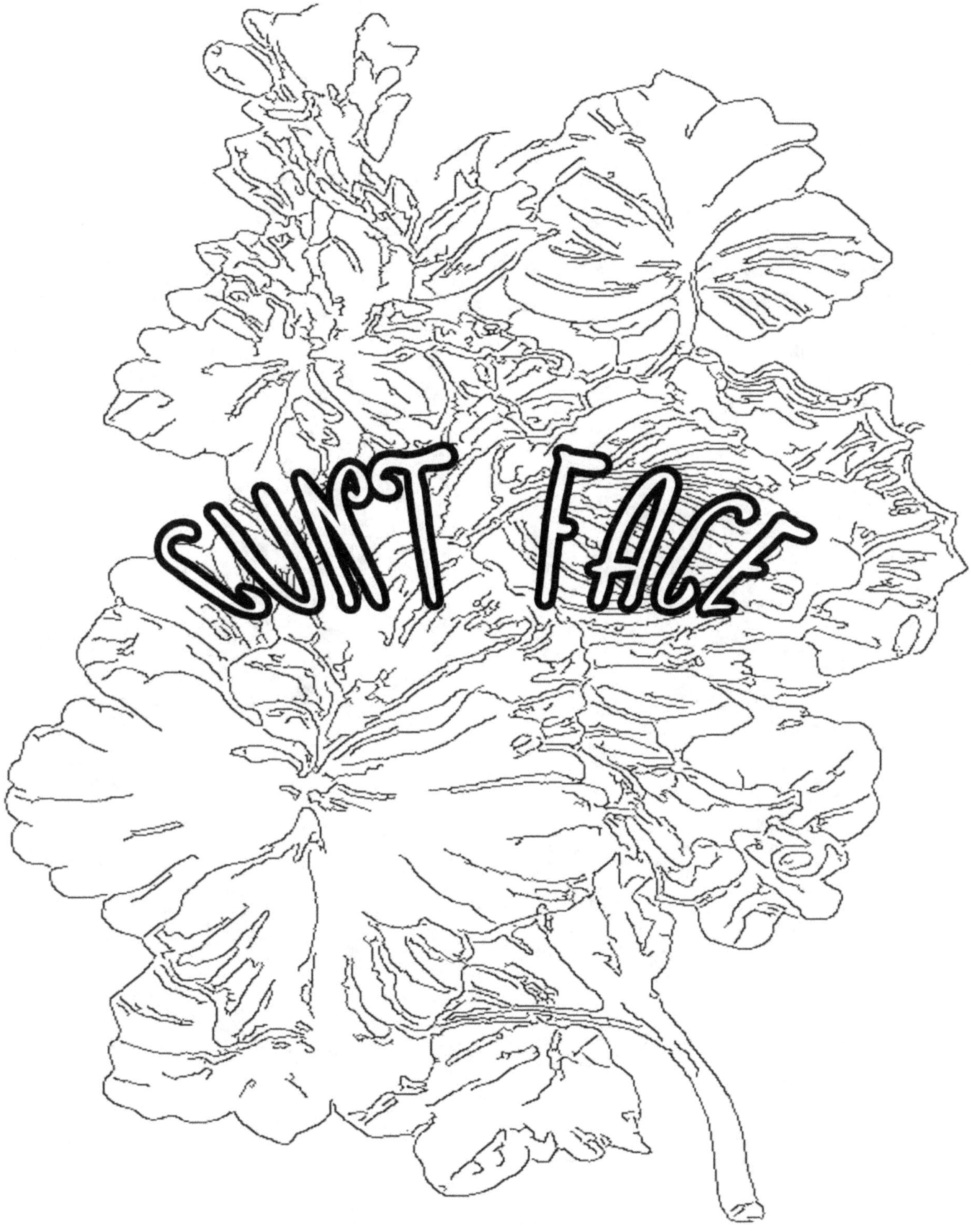
CUNT FACE

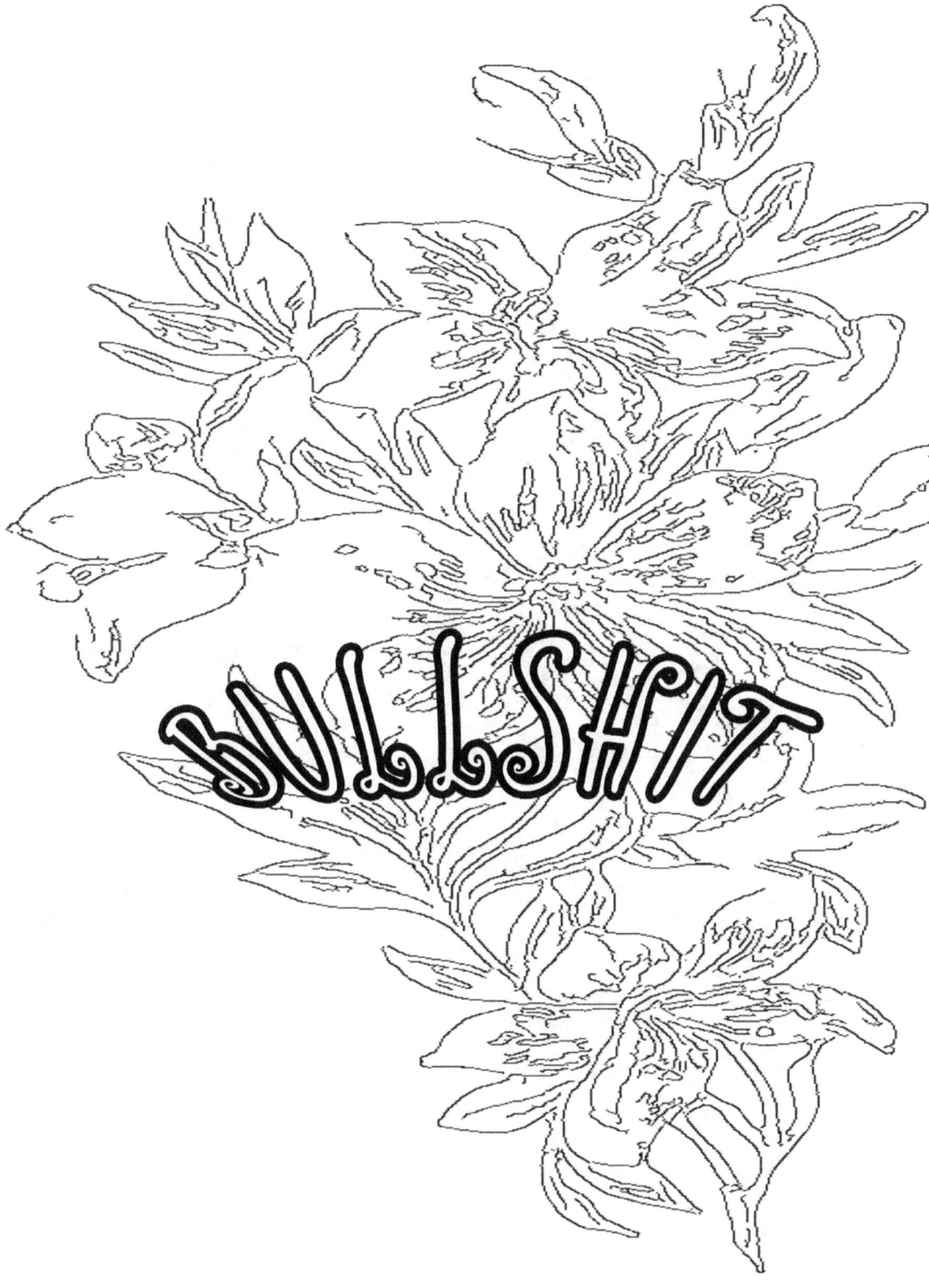
BULLSHIT

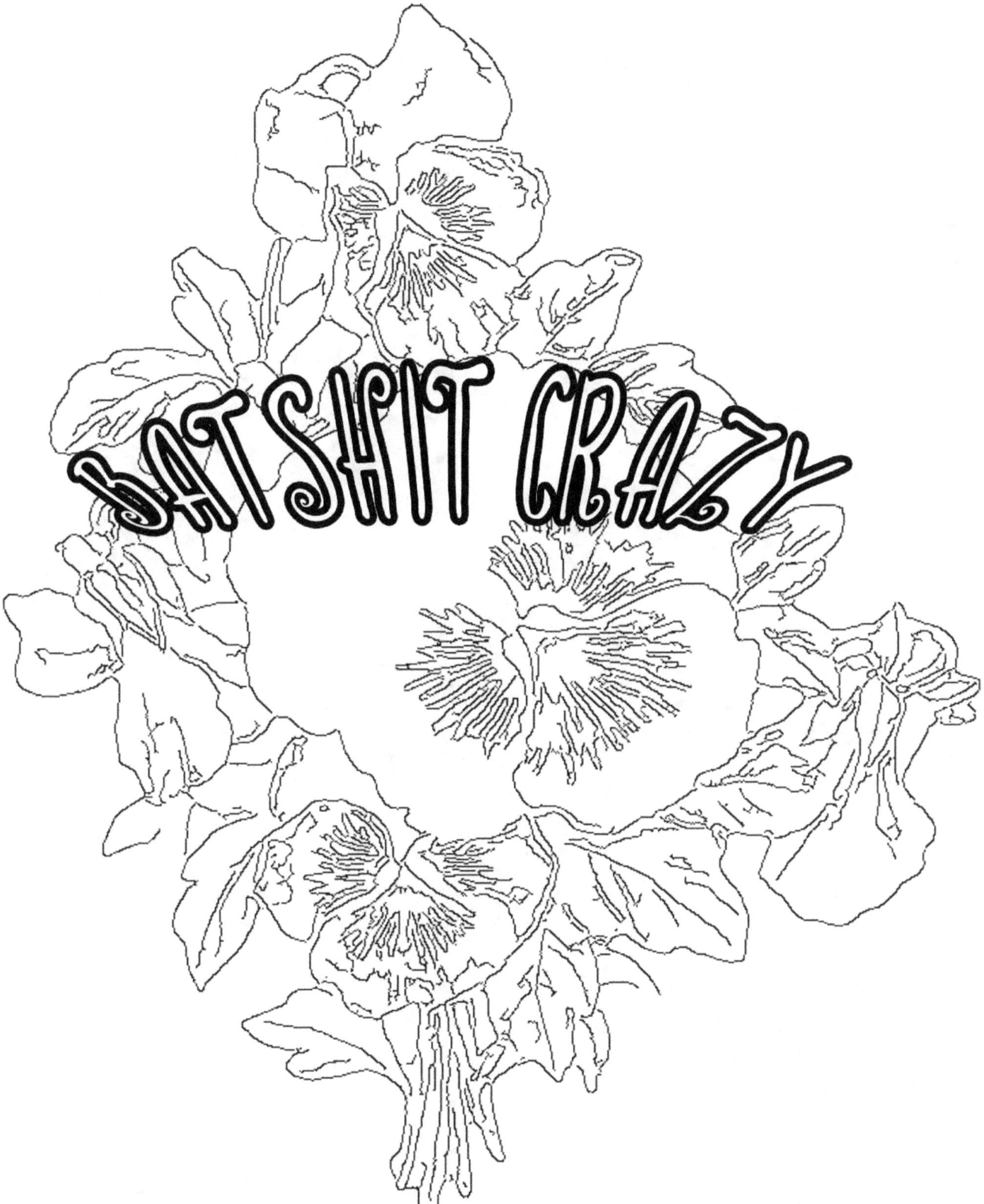
BATSHIT CRAZY

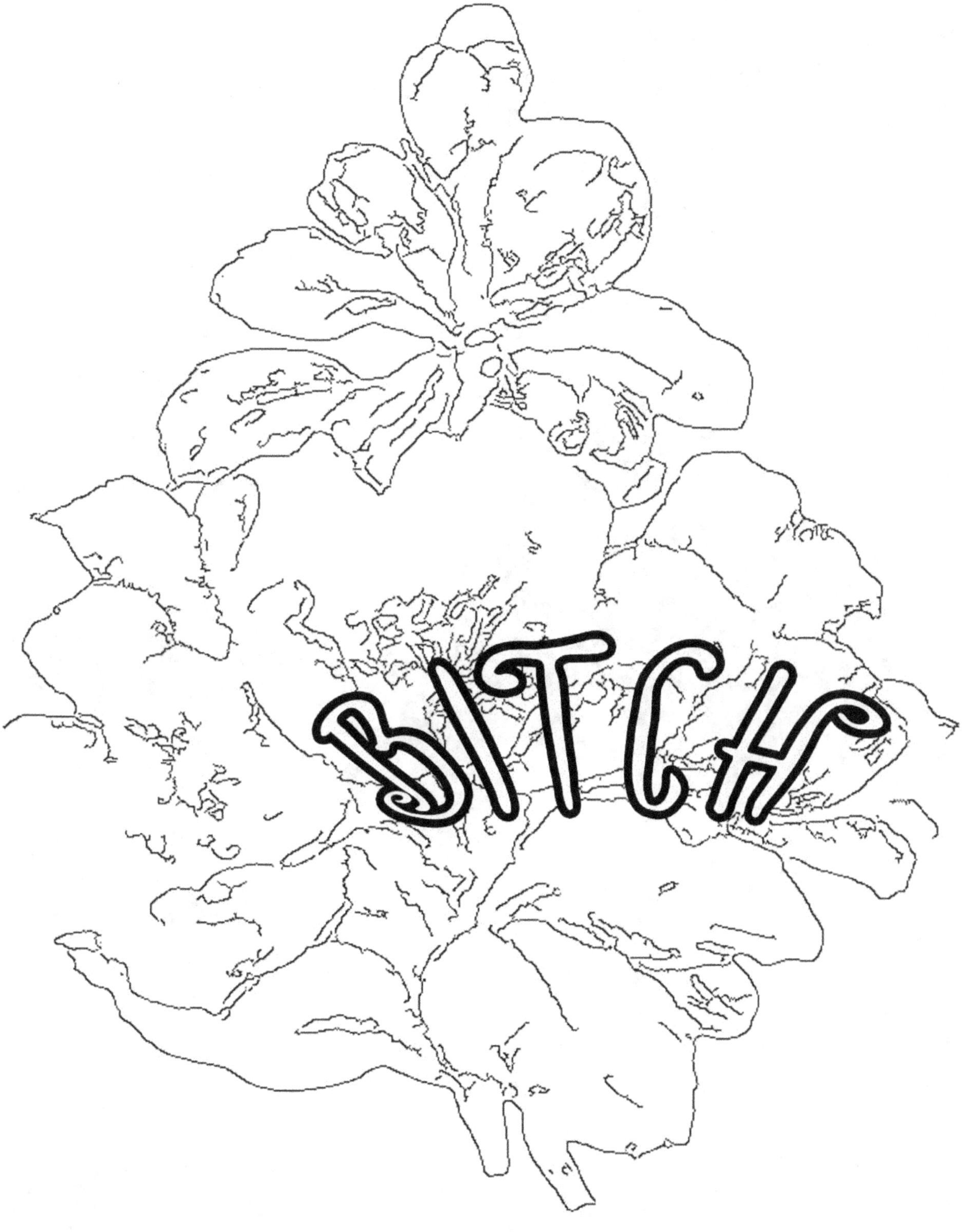
BITCH

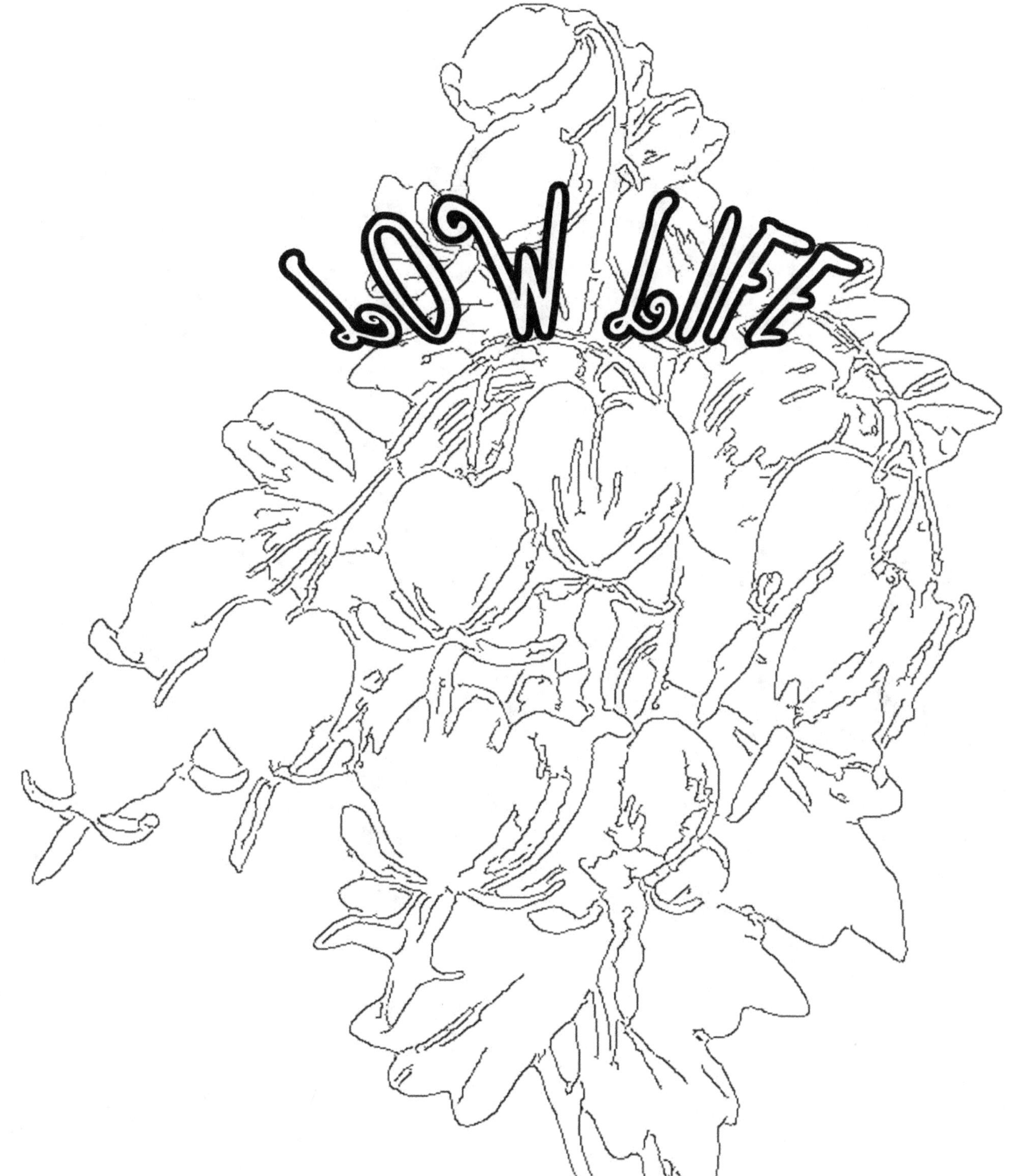
LOW LIFE

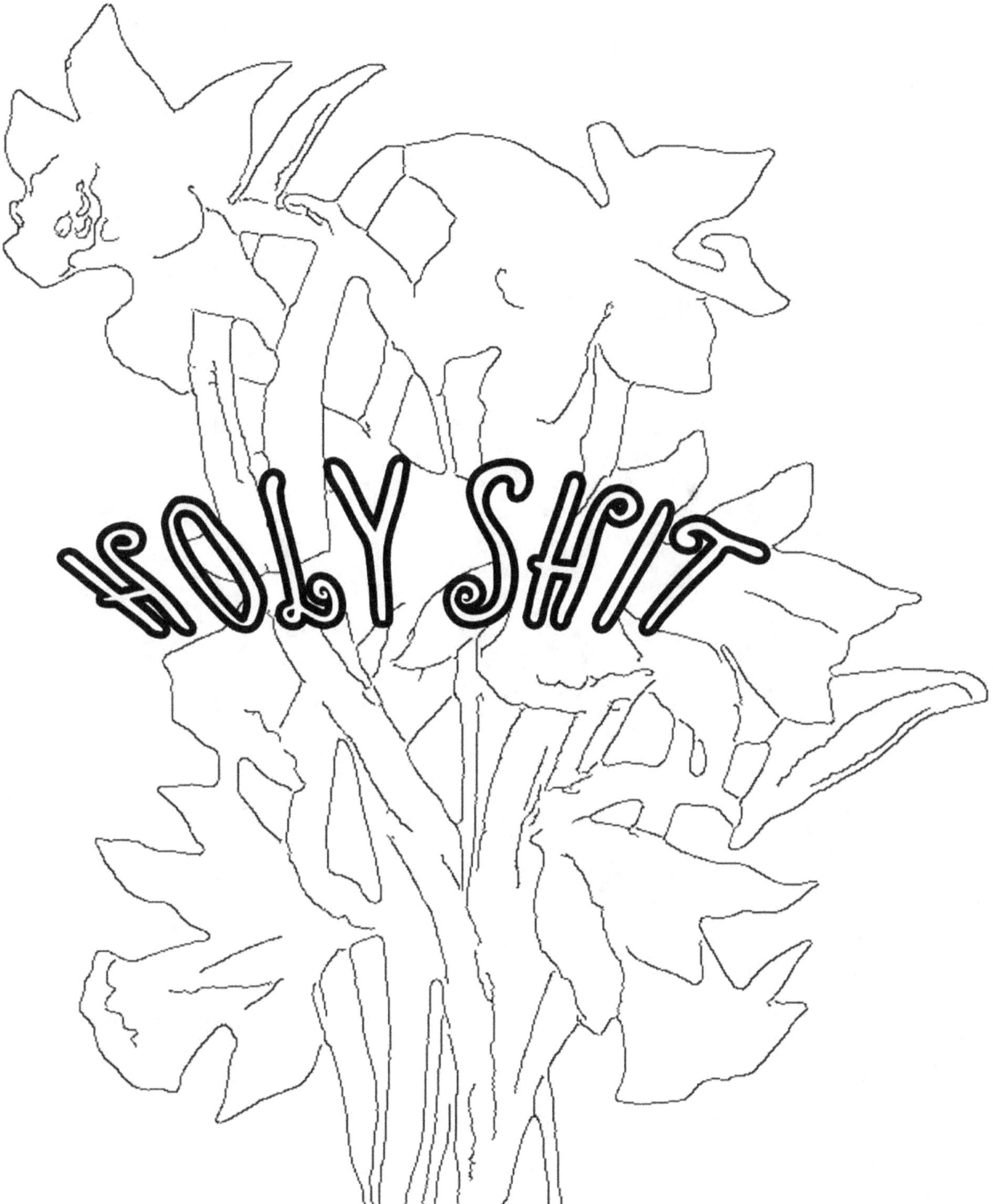
HOLY SHIT

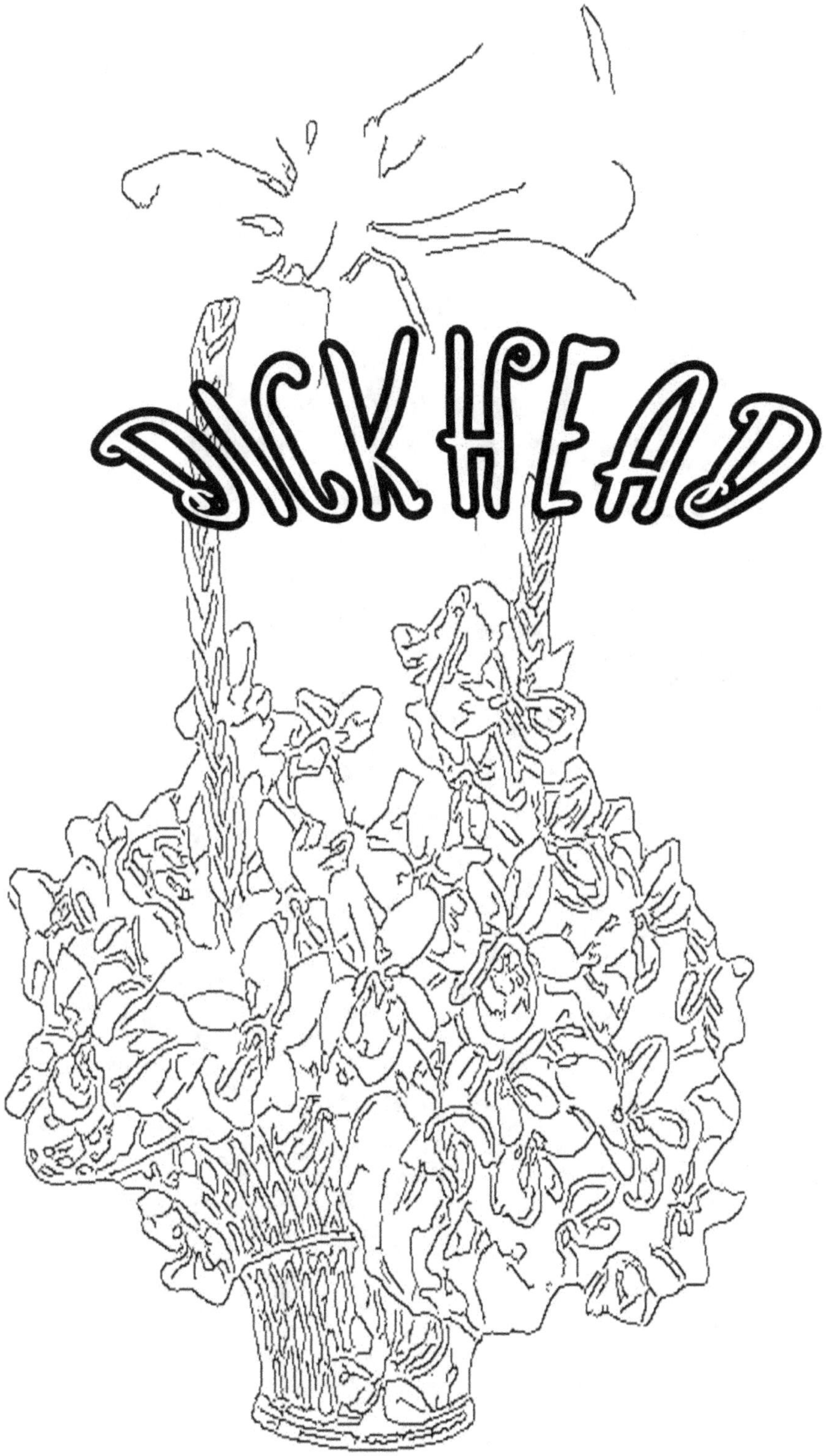
DICKHEAD

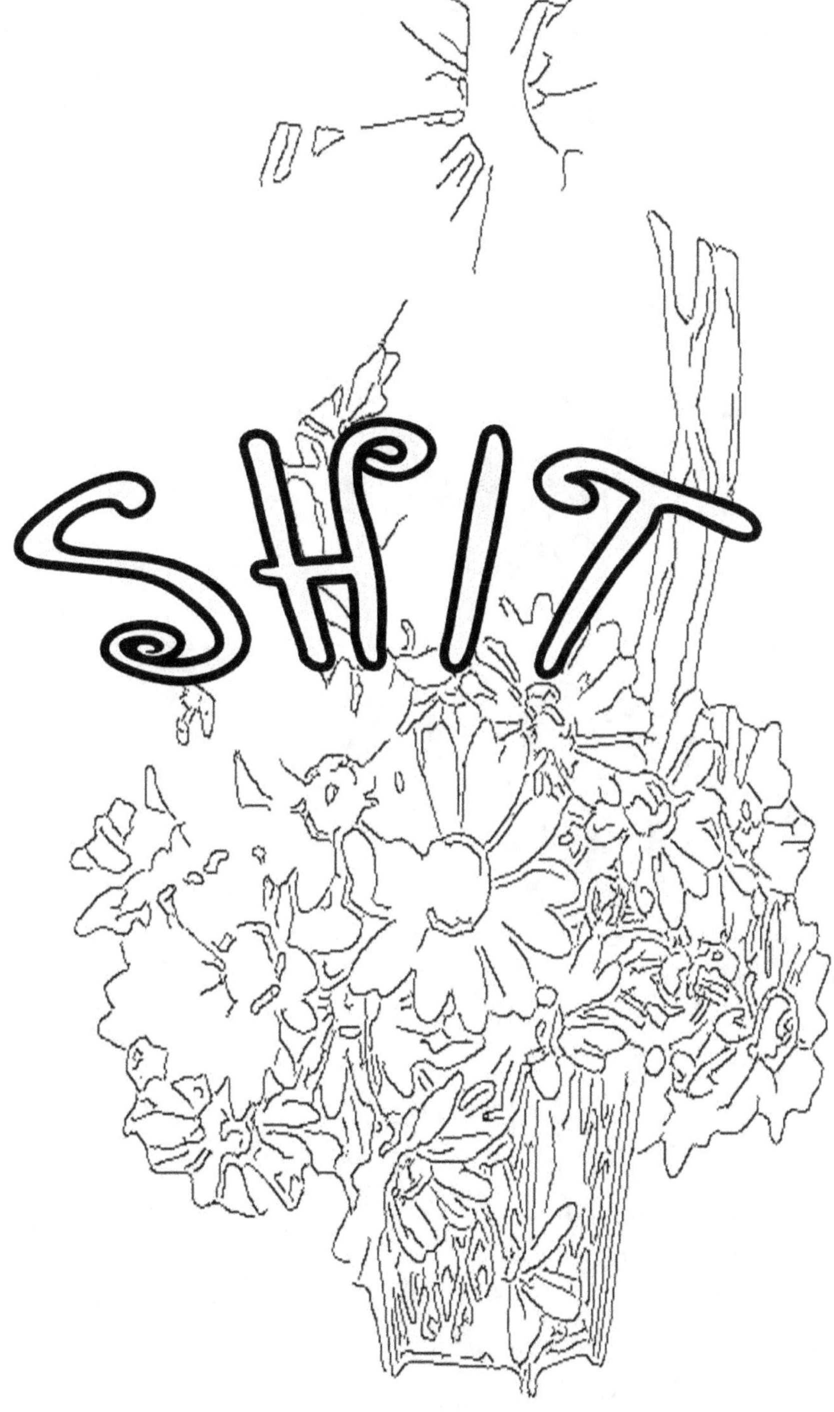
SHIT

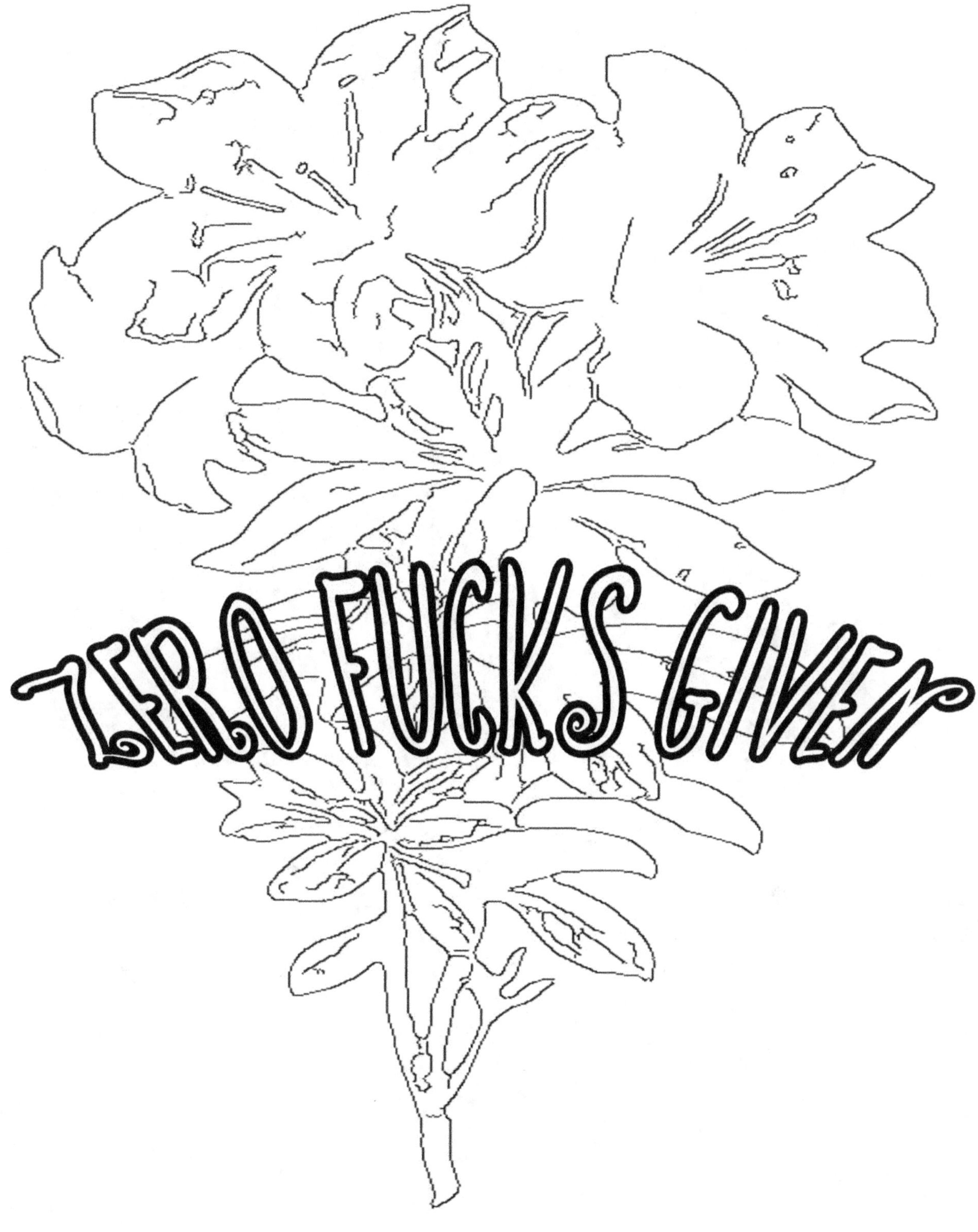
ZERO FUCKS GIVEN

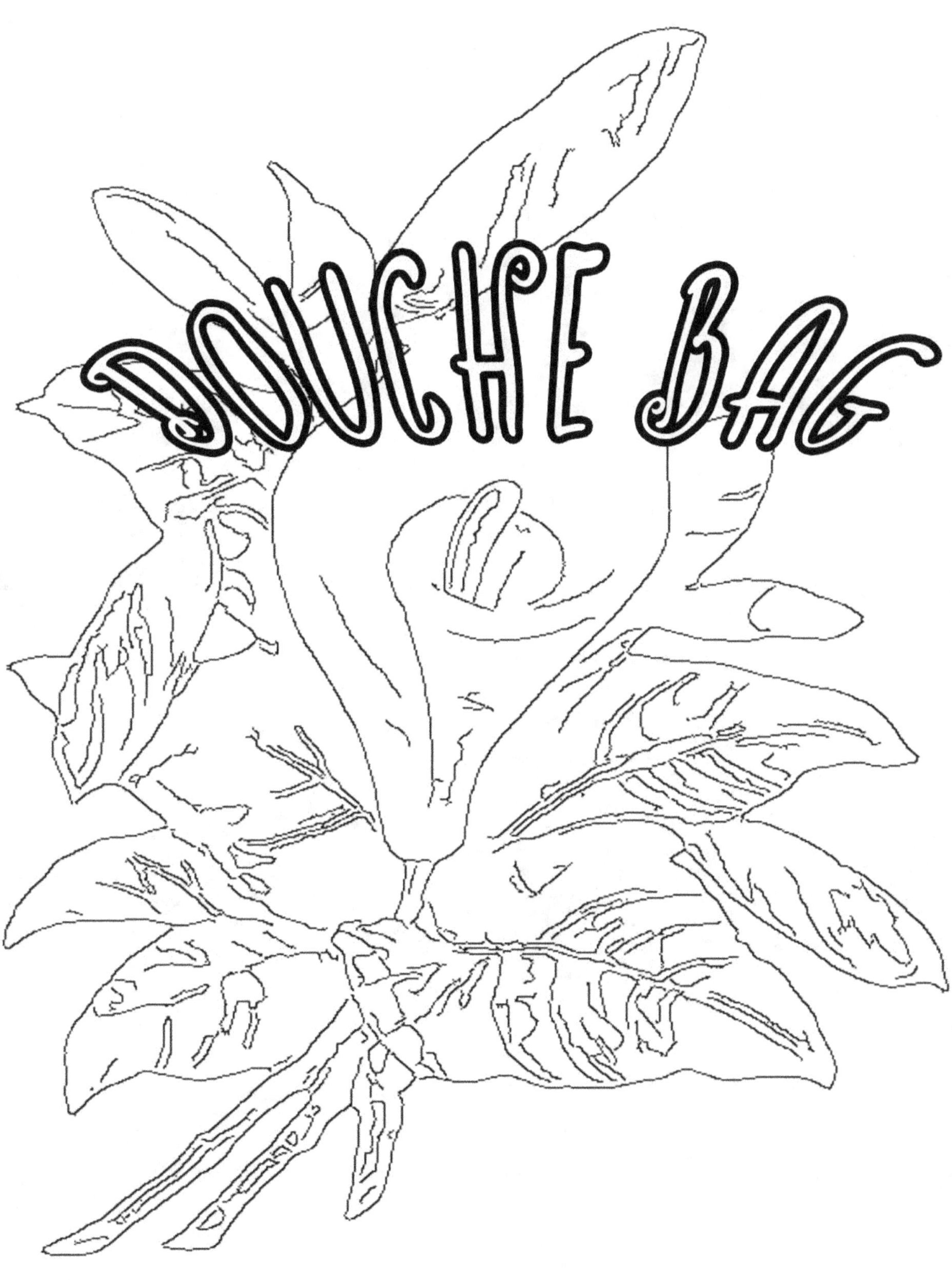
DOUCHE BAG

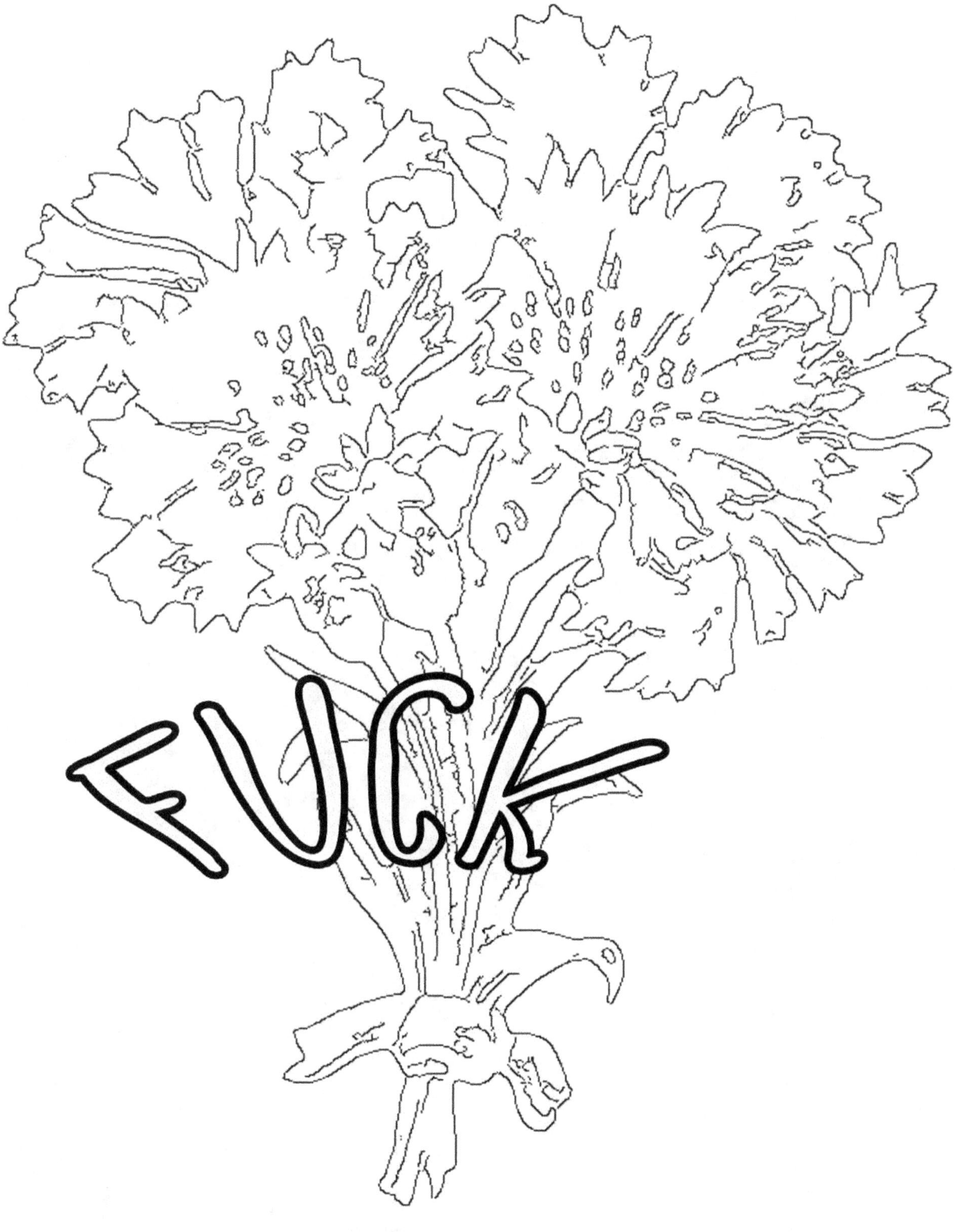
FUCK

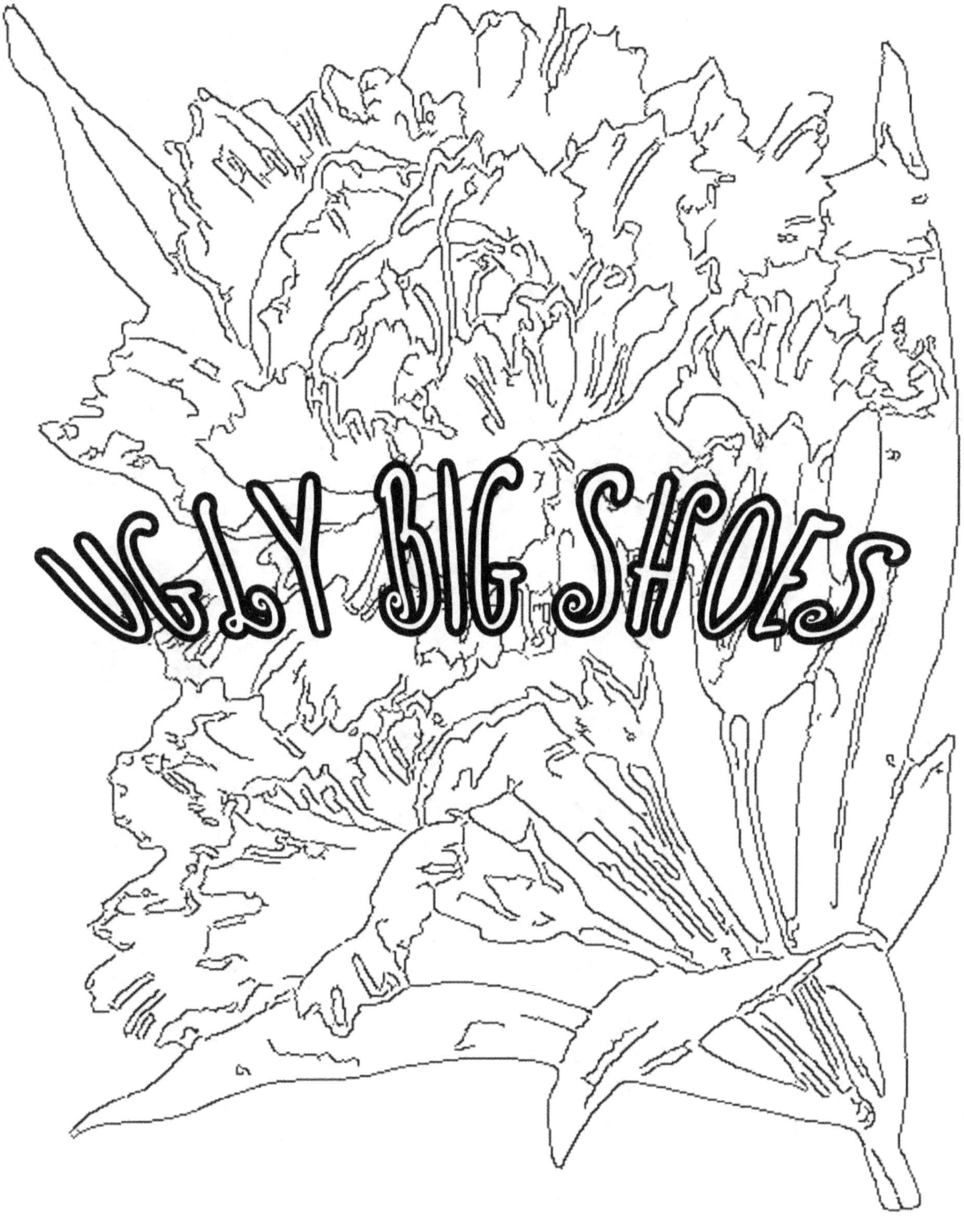
UGLY BIG SHOES

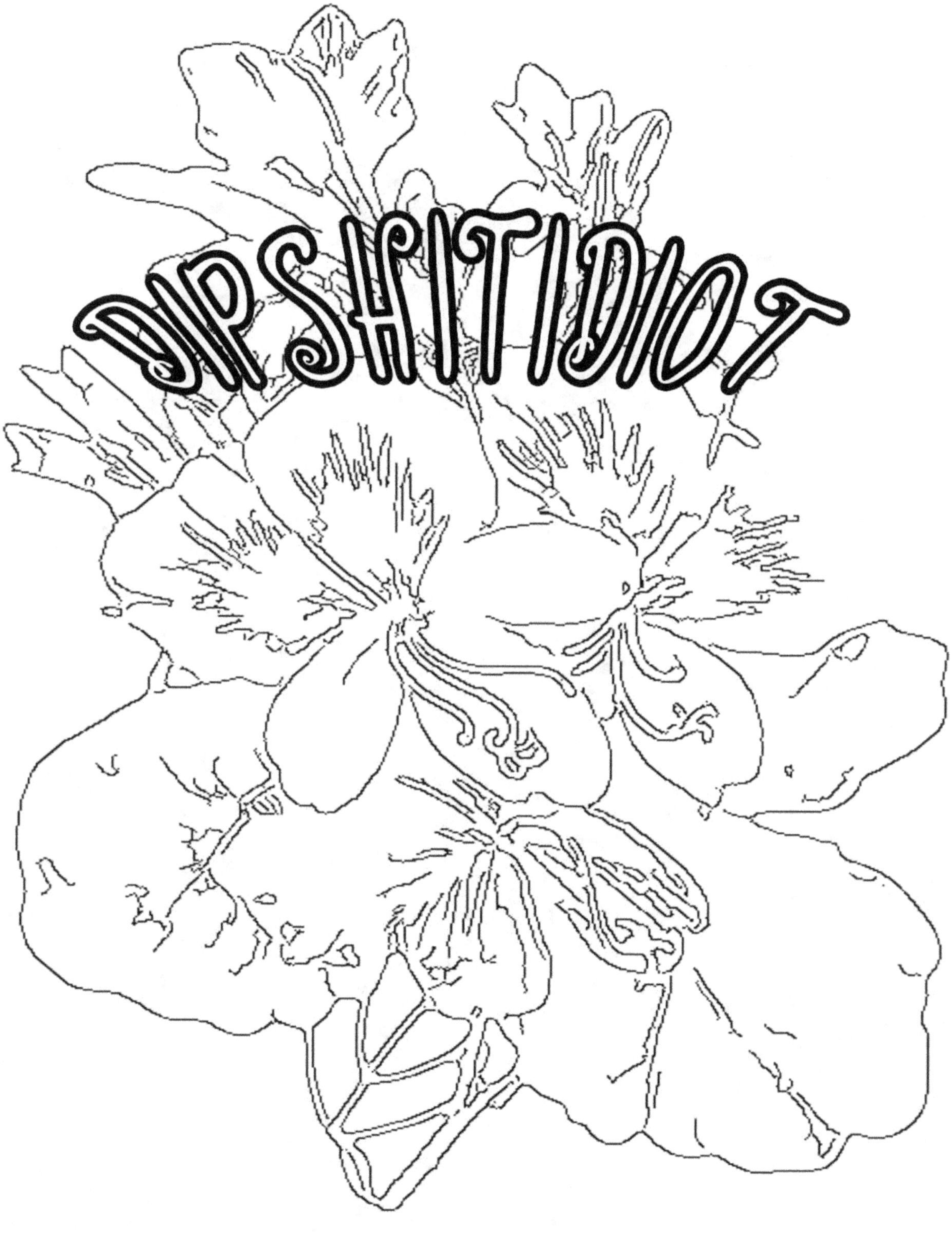
DIPSHITIDIOT

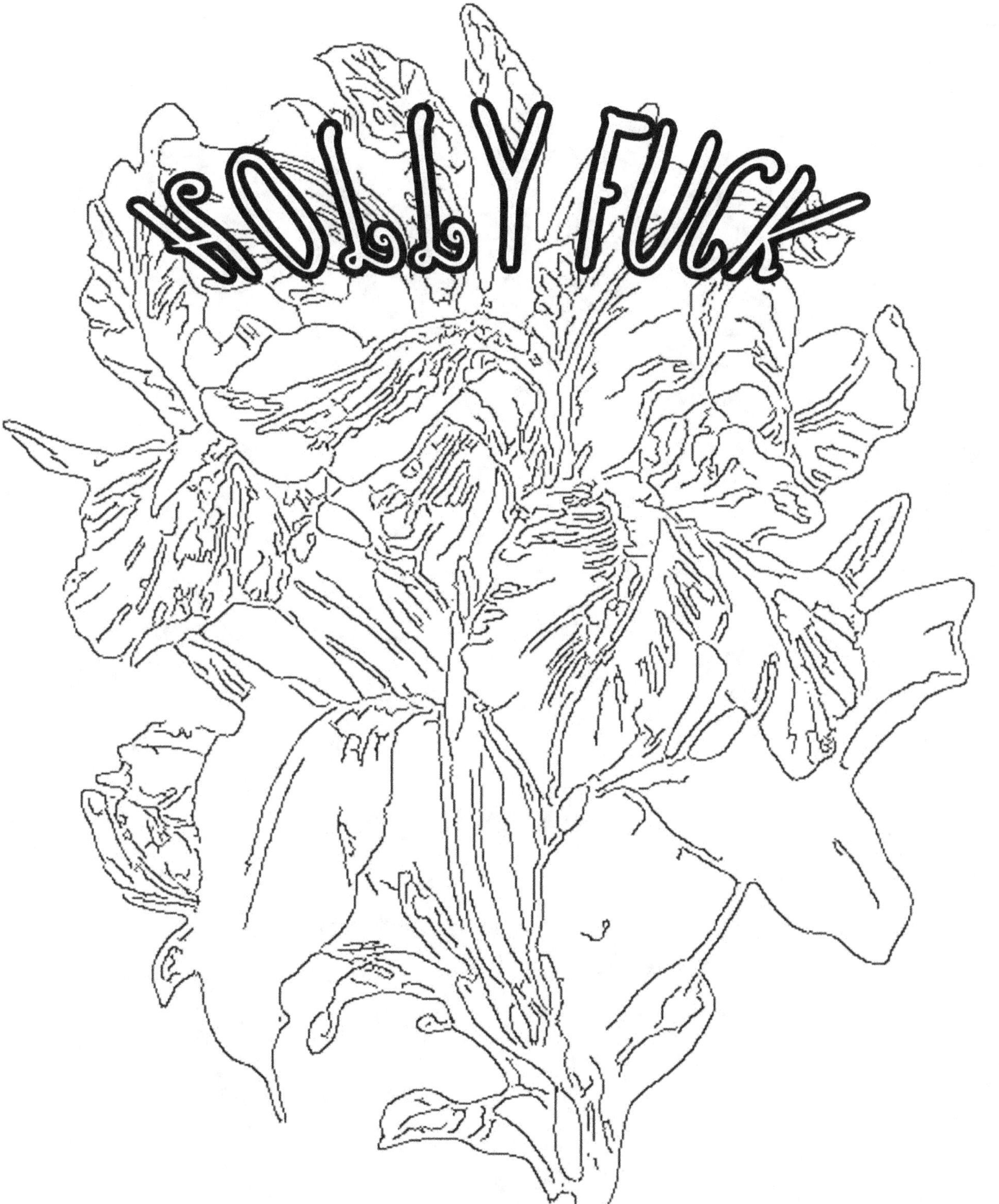
HOLLY FUCK

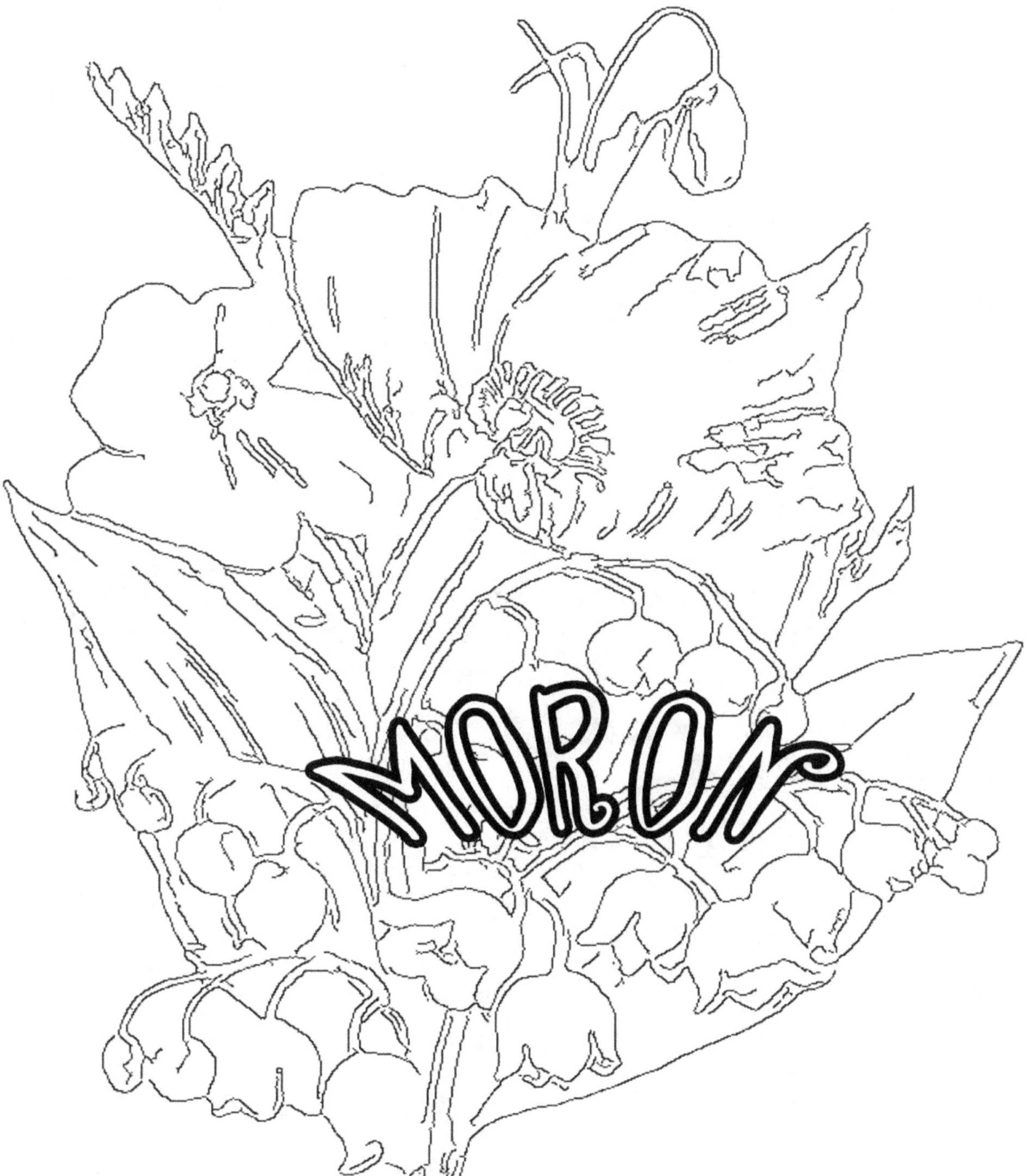
MORON

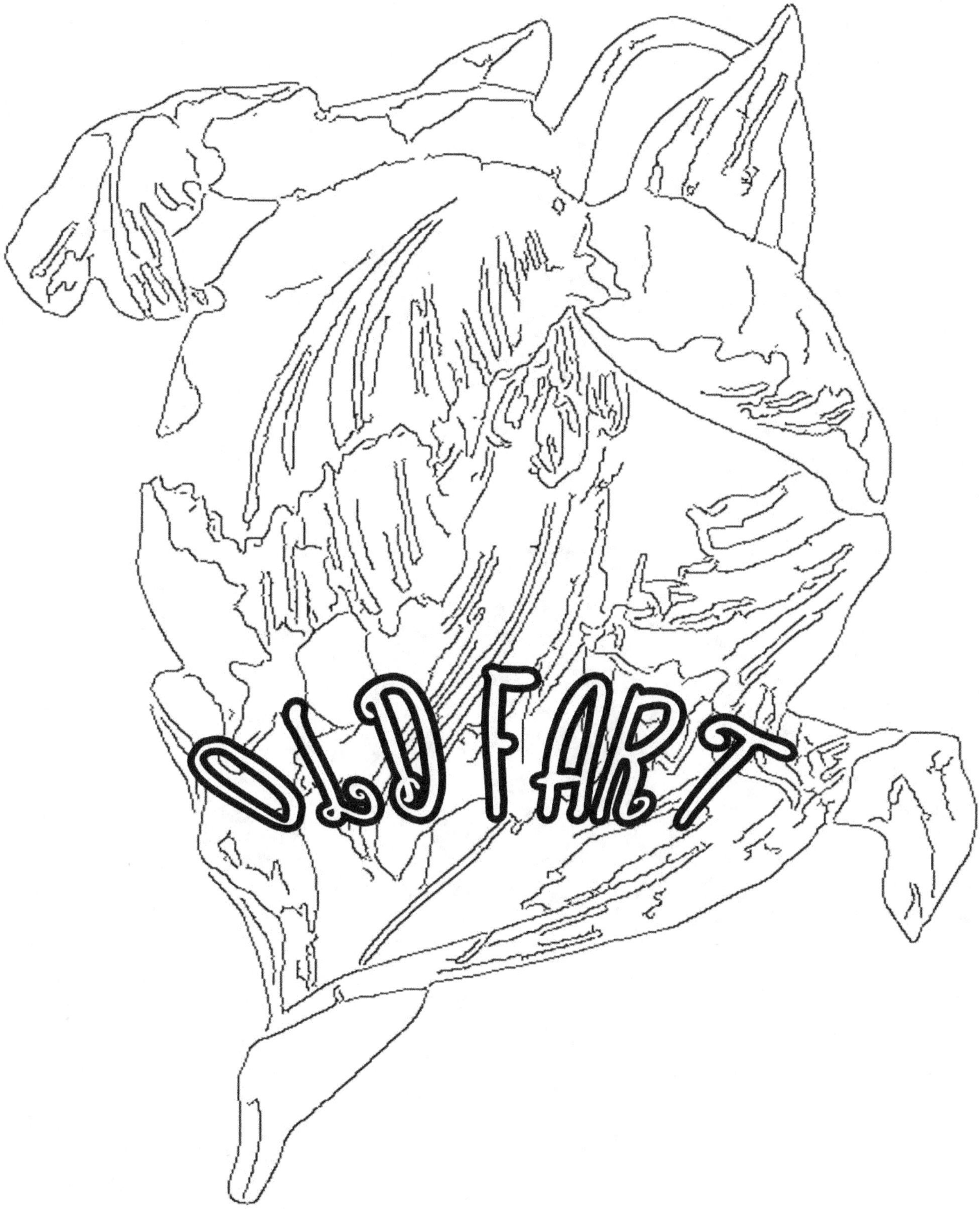
OLD FART

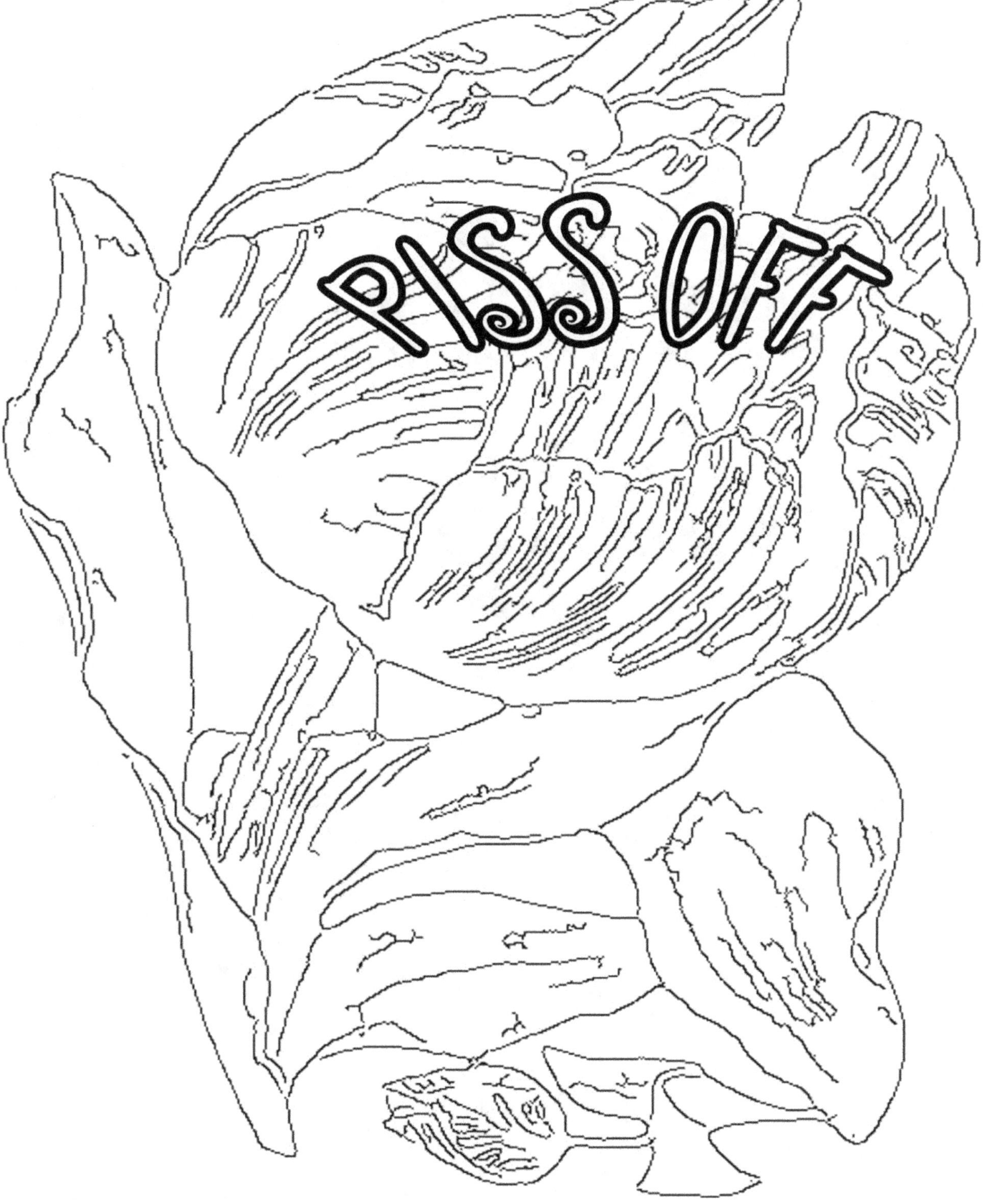
PISS OFF

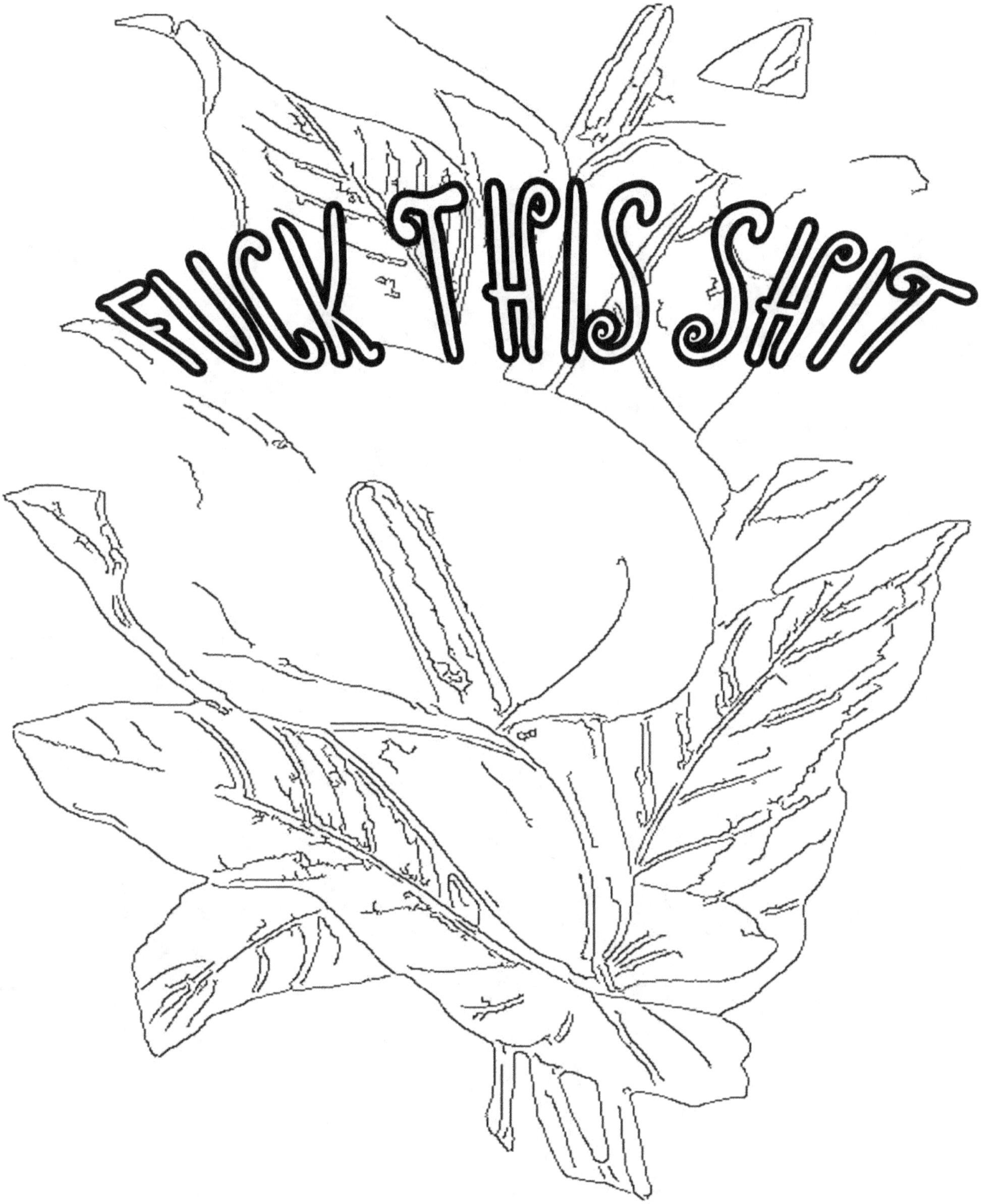
FUCK THIS SHIT

HAVE A GOOD DAY.

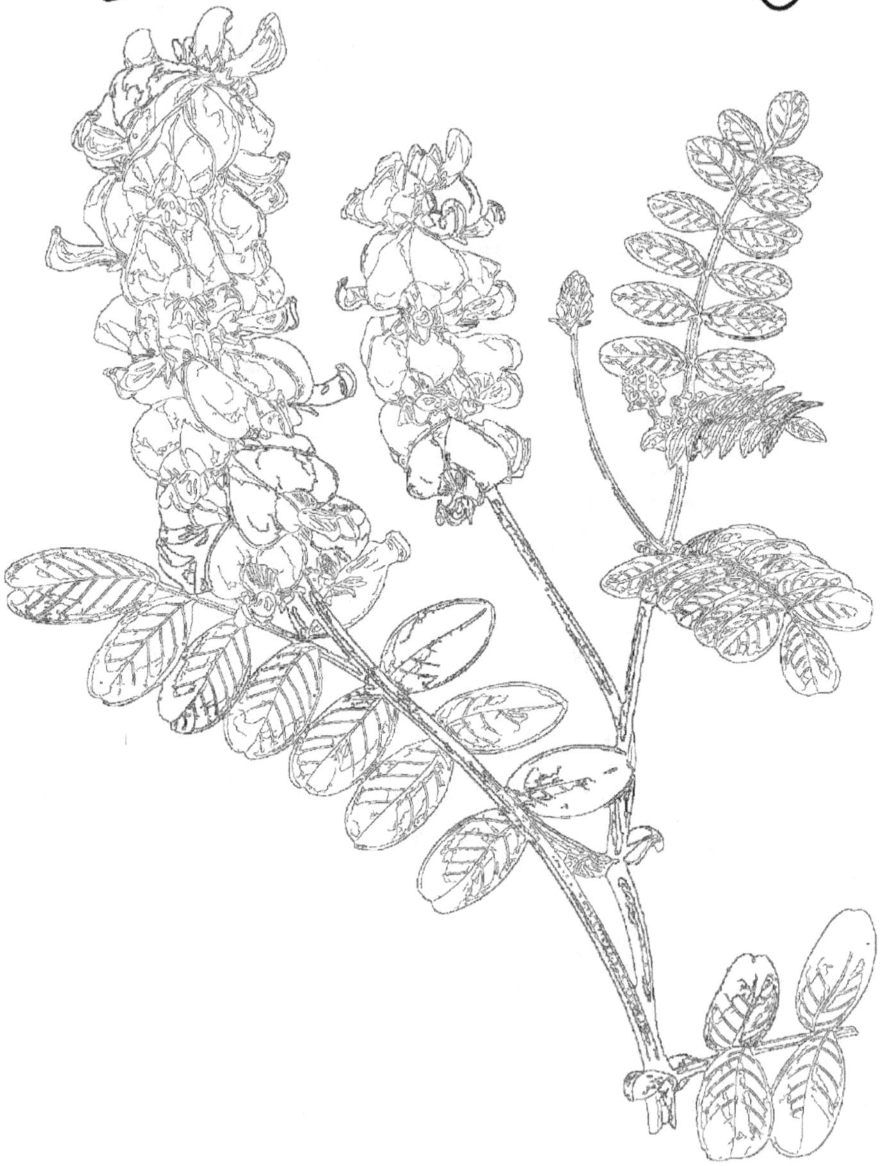

www.ingramcontent.com/pod-product-compliance
Lightning Source LLC
Chambersburg PA
CBHW081619220526
45468CB00010B/2940
9781983730931